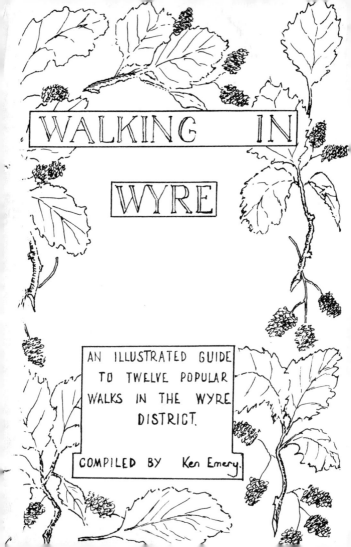

WALKING IN WYRE

WYRE

AN ILLUSTRATED GUIDE
TO TWELVE POPULAR
WALKS IN THE WYRE
DISTRICT.

COMPILED BY   Ken Emery.

04908905

Walking in Wyre
by Ken Emery

Published by Carnegie Publishing Ltd., 18 Maynard St.,
Ashton, Preston, Lancs PR2 2LS. Tel: (0772) 881246.

Printed by T. Snape & Co., Ltd., Boltons Court, Preston.

Walkers are advised to make use of the Ordnance Survey
Pathfinder or Landranger maps if they are in any doubt about
rights of way. They are also requested to respect the privacy of
the residents of the farmhouses, hamlets and homes which
these walks pass.

Any footpath obstruction should be notified to the County
Surveyor and Bridgemaster, County Hall, Preston.

INTRODUCTION.

This pocket-sized book is a pictorial guide to some twelve popular walks in Wyre

The district takes its name from the river which runs from the moorland and fells in the East of the region across the flat fertile North Fylde plain into the sea at Fleetwood. The area, therefore, offers a wide variety of beautiful countryside with many interesting towns and villages.

The walks have been chosen for their scenic value and for their interest. They are designed for the average family walker who wishes to explore this area and the use of a motor-car is assumed. For the country walks sensible footwear is advised.

The OS Landranger Map No.102 shows the numerous country lanes, paths and rights of way which can be used to modify these walks should you so require. Enjoy our beautiful countryside and please honour the Country Code.

Ken Emery. 1989.

THE COUNTRY CODE

Enjoy the countryside and respect its life and work.

Guard against all risk of fire.

Fasten all gates.

Keep your dogs under close control.

Keep to public paths across farmland.

Use gates and stiles to cross fences, hedges and walls.

Leave livestock, crops and machinery alone.

Take your litter home.

Help to keep all water clean.

Protect wild-life, plants and trees.

Take special care on country roads.

Make no unnecessary noise.

ACKNOWLEDGEMENTS

I acknowledge the help given to me by Mrs Joan Pendlebury of the Fleetwood Civic Society and by Mr Martin Ramsbottom for information on the "Fleetwood Town Trail"; by Mr Geoffrey Walker for notes on Brock Mill; by the British Waterways (Marketing Unit) for information on the Lancaster Canal and by my colleagues at the Wyre Borough Council for information and advice so readily given.

BIBLIOGRAPHY

A History of Pilling .... F. J. Sobee.

Fleetwood. A Town is Born...... "Bill" Curtis.

Fylde Regional Report......... Mawson.

Garstang and Over Wyre in Times Past.....
.... Catherine Rothwell.

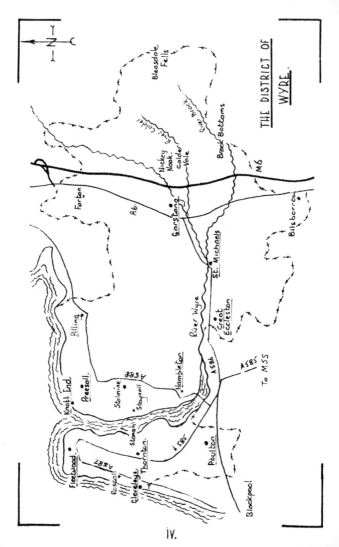

THE DISTRICT OF **WYRE.**

iV.

CONTENTS.

Walks in and around
THE WYRE ESTUARY.

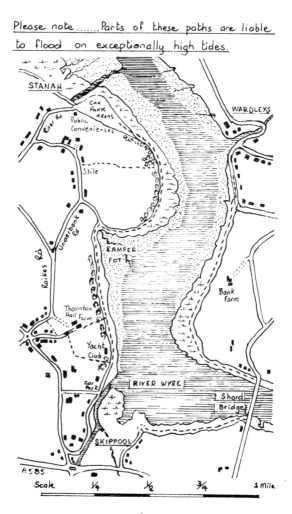

STANAH COUNTRY PARK TO RAMPER POT.

Here at Little Thornton, Hillylaid Pool discharges into the river at Stanah Clough. This watercourse is important in the drainage of a large area of Thornton and a huge screw pump lifts the water into the Wyre when flooding threatens.

Up to the turn of the century boats moored in the Clough bringing building materials and coal into Thornton.

In the 1960s the saltmarsh at Stanah was enclosed by an embankment and became the refuse tip for Thornton-Cleveleys. The reclaimed land is the large flat grassed area and parking bays now so popular with visitors.

In 1988 the Wyre Borough Council agreed to the creation of a country park at Stanah and to the improvement and waymarking of the network of footpaths in this region.

This walk starts here in the Country Park. Leave the car park and take the road across the park down to the riverside path.

WARDLEYS HOTEL, FERRY AND WAREHOUSES. (CIRCA 1940.)

After a few hundred yards we reach the site
of a cottage, rather grandly named
"Cockle Hall". From here you could whistle
the ferryman to take you across the river
to Wardleys. Of Cockle Hall all that is left
are a few fruit trees. Alas the ferry-
landing stage has long since disappeared
and you will have to walk upstream to
the Shard Bridge in order to cross
the river. Samphire, a local delicacy

which is gathered and pickled, grows on the saltmarsh hereabouts.

Half a mile further on we reach Ramper Pot and the moored boats at the yacht club at Skippool come into view. The name ramper derives from ramparts or banks built to protect land from flooding.

A return to the carpark at Stanah can be made by taking the track at the head of the pot and turning right along Underbank Road. On reaching the junction with River Rd. turn right to rejoin Stanah car-park.

A shorter route can be taken by using the public footpath from Underbank Road over the fields which joins the riverside path at the Cockle Hall site.

TOWARDS SKIPPOOL.

UNDERBANK ROAD.

6

STANAH COUNTRY PARK TO SKIPPOOL.

Leave the car-park at the Stanah Country Park and proceed along the riverside path to Ramper Pot as previously described.

The word "Wyre" comes from the celtic "Qwyr" which means pure or fresh. The Wyre differs from most rivers in that it narrows towards its mouth and consequently, at high water, a broad pool is formed between Fleetwood and Skippool. On Speed's map of Lancashire published in 1611, this stretch of water was named "Bergerode" which means safe anchorage.

On reaching Ramper Pot we carry on down the riverside path passing a line of moored boats, the yacht club-house and the "River House" restaurant and soon reach the car-park. Opposite is the Thornton-Cleveleys Cricket Club ground where refreshments can usually be obtained on Saturday afternoons and most Sundays, during the cricket season.

YACHT CLUB, SKIPPOOL

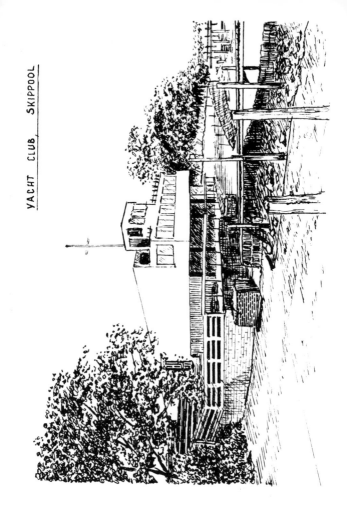

There is evidence that man has known the Skippool area for many centuries; flint implements and bronze age pottery have been found here. There was a reference to Skippool in 1330 when, in the reign of Edward III, a road was granted from Poulton passing "Skeppol". There was trade through Skippool as early as 1590. In 1744 Poulton was considered a port through its operation at Skippool. With the emergence of Fleetwood in 1840, Skippool's commercial importance declined. Today the whole area has been taken over by yachtsmen and those who like "messing about on the river."

To return to Stanah you can retrace your steps along the riverside path. Alternatively, take the path at the side of the yacht club-house across the fields to Thornton Hall Farm turning left down the access lane to a stile on your right. Take this short path to Raikes Road turning right along this road and then down Underbank Road at the fork. At Ramper Pot the route is as described on page 5.

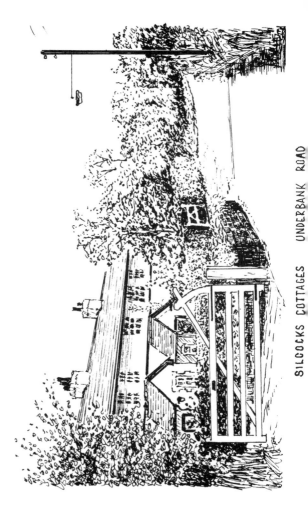

SILCOCKS COTTAGES   UNDERBANK ROAD

SKIPPOOL TO WARDLEYS

"Wellies" or waterproof boots are the order of the day for this walk. Do not proceed at very high tides as parts of the path will flood.

Leave the carpark at Skippool, turn right up Wyre Road and, passing Thornton Lodge, turn left up Skippool Road to the roundabout on the A585. Bearing left we cross over two watercourses. The second is shown on Speed's map of 1611 as "Skippon Flue"; now canalized it is called "Main Dyke" and drains a large area of the Fylde, its source being "Marton Mere", east of Blackpool. Turning left down Old Mains Lane go through the last gate on the left and, turning right, the path is picked up descending the embankment to the riverside.

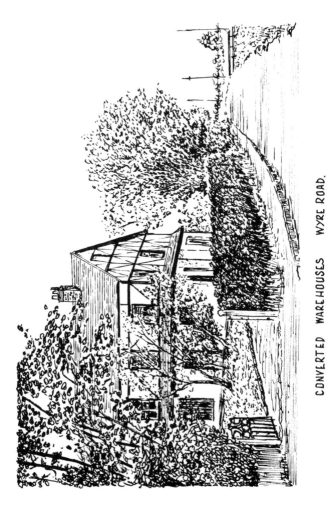

CONVERTED WAREHOUSES   WYRE ROAD.

Take the riverside path to Shard Bridge and, after paying your toll — one penny - cross over the river.

The bridge, built in 1864, is on the site of one of many fords which crossed the river. "Aldwarth" is the old name for Shard, (Allt - stream, Wath a ford) It is planned to build a new bridge in the near future as the present structure is becoming uneconomical to maintain.

We continue the walk by rejoining the riverside path access to which is provided by a slipway at the end of the bridge. Now walking downstream the view towards Skippool is quite spectacular. At Point Shard the path follows the river bank through 90 degrees and Ramper Pot comes into view. The path goes along the top of a flood embankment and Wardleys, our destination, is in sight. At Saltmarsh Lane the path descends to the marsh again to join a rough track which takes us to Wardleys Creek where the metalled road leads us to the Wardleys Hotel, the end of our walk.

Unless alternative arrangements have been made, we retrace our steps back to Skippool.

SHARD BRIDGE.

14

Like Skippool, Wardleys was once an important centre of commerce before the establishment of Fleetwood. It was part of the port of Poulton and in 1708 there were three pilots at Knott End

WARDLEYS HOTEL

who could give safe passage to Wardleys. The warehouses were built in 1825, to be pulled down in 1972. They housed cotton and flax, part of the Baltic trade, which was used at the mills at Kirkham. Later they were used to store guano. The Wardleys Hotel was built over two hundred years ago and was then known as the Royal Oak. Four hundred years ago a cottage served as the local hostelry and it was known as the Ship Inn.

Again like Skippool all commercial sailing has ceased and the area is now a busy marina.

The word Wardleys derives from the Anglo-Saxon "worth" - a warded place; "Leag" a field.

WARDLEYS CREEK.

A WALK FROM CLEVELEYS TO FLEETWOOD (and back by tram).

A WALK - CLEVELEYS TO FLEETWOOD -

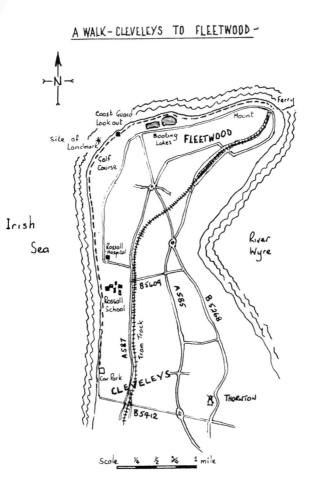

Scale ¼ ½ ¾ 1 mile

A WALK FROM CLEVELEYS TO FLEETWOOD
FOUR AND THREE QUARTER MILES (and back by tram — "a tramp and a tram!!")

This walk takes us right along the top of the coastal sea defences and, as we walk, we should reflect on the awesome power of the sea and man's attempts to keep it at bay. This route is a long established right of way but, be warned, do not exercise your right during storm conditions at high tide.

Our walk starts from the large free car-park behind the bathing chalets on the promenade at Cleveleys. Heading north along the promenade you may be able to observe what appear to be banks of mud at low tide on the beach at Cleveleys. Close examination will reveal that they are, in fact, peat indicating that this was once land covered with trees and vegetation. The coast-line as shown on John Speed's map in 1610, allowing for inaccuracies, was between ½ and ¾ of a mile out to sea. After about

half a mile we reach the playing fields of
Rossall School.

Rossall

Ancient forms - Rushale, Rosholl - thought to
derive from the Celtic word "Rhos" - a moor.

The site of the original Manor House has
now long been engulfed by the sea. During the
15th and 16th century Rossall was owned by the
Abbey of Salop and leased to the Abbey and
Convent of Deulacres in Staffordshire. It was
tenanted by George Allen, cousin of the Abbot
of Deulacres, whose younger grandson was the
famous Cardinal William Allen (1532-94) who was
born and brought up at Rossall. When the
Cardinal's elder brother, Richard, died in 1583, his
widow and three daughters refused to give up
the old religion and fled to the Cardinal's
protection at Rheims. Rossall passed to Edmund
Fleetwood whose father, Thomas, had purchased
the reversion of the lease from Henry VIII at
the Dissolution. Thence it descended through
the Fleetwoods and the Fleetwood-Heskeths

until Sir Peter Hesketh-Fleetwood (1801-66) gave it to Rossall School in 1844. Rossall Hall stood on the site of the school dining hall and the gazebo, which was built in its grounds, still stands. It was built either by Richard Fleetwood who died in 1709 or his son, Edward, who died in 1737.

THE GAZEBO ROSSALL SCHOOL

Continuing our walk we soon reach Rossall Hospital. On the beach immediately in front of the sea-wall can be seen huge pieces of concrete being the debris resulting from a breach in the wall which occurred in 1954 A plaque on the top of the approach to the wall commemorates the completion and strengthening of the Fleetwood coastal defences between 1927 and 1961. Following serious flooding in 1977 further work was carried out all along the coast from Fleetwood to Cleveleys.

Major inundations have been recorded in the past.

1532. Village, Waddum Thorpe, destroyed.

1555. Destruction of village, Singleton Thorpe, site now well out to sea south of Cleveleys

1720. Large areas of Fylde coast flooded.

1771, 1796. Areas of land lost.

1833. As the result the first attempts at sea defence made in the Fleetwood area

1863. The 1833 earthen defences swept away, rebuilt with timber hulking

1927. Fleetwood flooded, loss of six lives.

1938 Repairs to wall at Cleveleys.

1954 Major breach plugged at Rossall.

1977 Large areas at Fleetwood, Rossall and Cleveleys flooded, extensive damage to property.

BEACH OPPOSITE HOSPITAL.

Past the Hospital there is a mile walk along a straight section of the wall until we reach the Fleetwood Golf Course. Note the lagoon and drainage on the land side of the wall. These are designed to catch any wave-spray water blown over the top of the wall which can happen at high tide at times of strong winds.

The coast-line changes direction at Rossall Point and we now head in a North-Easterly direction. At Rossall Point, until the early part of this century, there stood a large wooden navigational structure called The Landmark. All the early maps show it clearly and a similar structure existed on this site when the Domesday Book was compiled between 1084 and 1086. The timber hulks which formed the base can sometimes be seen protruding from the beach just beyond groyne 56 (numbered on the wall.) The circular base is about 19yds in diameter and by close examination of early

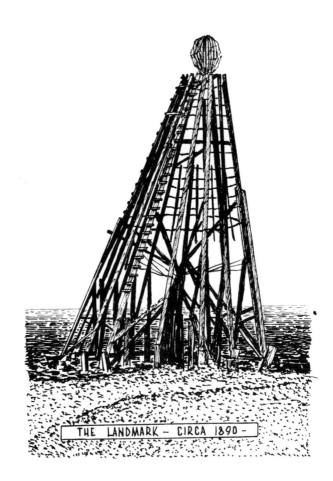

THE LANDMARK - CIRCA 1890 -

26

photographs I estimate that it would have stood, at least, 75 ft above ground level.

A more modern structure associated with the sea is the Coastguards' Lookout Station which we pass next on our walk to Fleetwood.

On a clear day the view across the bay is spectacular with the Lake District Mountains providing a magnificent back drop to the scene. Why not stop and identify their silhouettes?

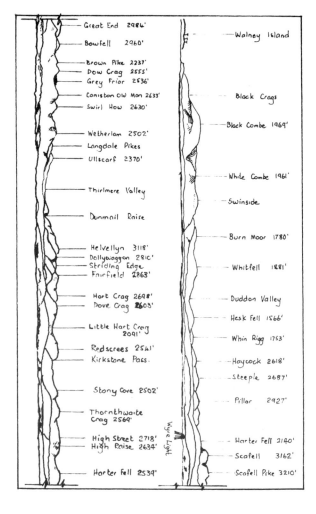

Great End 2984'
Bowfell 2960'

Brown Pike 2237'
Dow Crag 2555'
Grey Friar 2536'
Coniston Old Man 2633'
Swirl How 2630'

Wetherlam 2502'
Langdale Pikes
Ullscarf 2370'

Thirlmere Valley

Dunmail Raise

Helvellyn 3118'
Dollywaggon 2810'
Striding Edge
Fairfield 2863'

Hart Crag 2698'
Dove Crag 2603'

Little Hart Crag 2091'

Redscrees 2541'
Kirkstone Pass.

Stony Cove 2502'

Thornthwaite Crag 2569'

High Street 2718'
High Raise 2634'

Harter Fell 2539'

Walney Island

Black Crags

Black Combe 1969'

White Combe 1961'

Swinside

Burn Moor 1780'

Whitfell 1881'

Duddon Valley

Hesk Fell 1566'

Whin Rigg 1753'

Haycock 2618'

Steeple 2687'

Pillar 2927'

Wyre Light

Harter Fell 2140'

Scafell 3162'

Scafell Pike 3210'

28

29

Walking on we pass the Boating Lake, the Marine Hall and Gardens, the Pier and finally arrive at the tram terminus opposite the Ferry.

The Trams.

Blackpool Corporation agreed to the construction of a line along their promenade in 1884. This was added to and converted from conduit power collection to overhead wires by 1899. The Blackpool and Fleetwood Tramroad Co. built a line from Fleetwood to Blackpool along the cliff tops, the terminus being the Talbot Rd. Railway Station, now Blackpool North, in 1898. In 1919 the Corporation purchased this company and its 41 single deck tramcars and two depots at Copse Rd. Fleetwood and Red Bank Rd. Bispham. In 1963 the route along Dickson Rd to Blackpool North Station was discontinued following the abandonment of all the street tramways in Blackpool. Today the coastal route is still in operation and carries many passengers. Fleetwood now remains the only town in the Country to have a tramway operate along its main street. Every year on a Sunday in July the main street is closed to normal traffic when the Tram and Transport Festival is held. Many of the old trams, now restored, are on display along with other vintage forms of transport.

To conclude our expedition we catch a tram and book the fare to Cleveleys. On the journey back note the old earth banks between Rossall Lane and Rossall Beach built to protect the farmers' fields from the sea.

On arriving at Cleveleys head up Victoria Road West to the sea-front and thence to the car-park, our place of departure.

FLEETWOOD — A TOWN TRAIL

FLEETWOOD TOWN TRAIL (APPROX. 1½ Miles.)

FLEETWOOD — A TOWN TRAIL.

Introduction

Fleetwood is a young town, being founded by Sir Peter Hesketh-Fleetwood who inherited the Rossall Estate in 1824. He commissioned Decimus Burton, a London architect, to plan the town on the wild, wind-swept, isolated rabbit warren at the mouth of the River Wyre. Decimus Burton laid out the plan of the town using the Mount, then known as Tup Hill, as the centre from which the streets would radiate. He borrowed a plough with which he marked the fields to indicate the new town's street plan. 1840 saw the railway link with Preston and travellers were able to embark on ships to the Lakes, Dublin, Belfast, Ardrossan and the Isle of Man. The rail link was discontinued in 1970. Fleetwood became a major fishing port and the town prospered. With the decline of the fishing industry the port developed "roll on-roll off" trade with Ireland. At the present time there are ambitious plans to develop the docks as a marina and leisure complex.

1 Cottages - Abbotts Walk.

These cottages are some of the earliest buildings in Fleetwood and were originally occupied by the coastguards. In those days before the sea defences were built, the cottages would have been very

near to the high-water mark and the coastguards would have enjoyed an uninterrupted view down the channel and out to sea.

THE MOUNT PAVILION.

36

2. The Mount

The original Chinese pavilion which adorned the summit was designed by Decimus Burton and was replaced by the present structure in 1902. The clock was presented to the town by Mr Isaac Spencer in 1919 to the memory of Fleetwood men who lost their lives in the first world war. The building is now occupied as a craft centre to which the public are admitted and the movement of the clock can be examined. The views from the Mount are spectacular on a clear day.

3. The Lighthouses.

The Lower Lighthouse and the Pharos Lighthouse are so arranged that when the two are aligned, the channel can be safely navigated. Designed by Burton, they were switched on in December 1840. The Lower Lighthouse stands 30 ft. above high water level and its light is visible for 9 miles, Pharos Light stands 90 ft. above high water level and is visible for 13 miles.

THE PHAROS LIGHTHOUSE.

4. North Euston Hotel.

At the time the hotel was built in 1841 Fleetwood was on the shortest route, via rail and sea, between London and Glasgow and it was expected that the hotel would be well used by travellers. It was designed by Decimus Burton for Sir Peter Hesketh-Fleetwood and the first manager, a Corsican, Xenon Vantini, was a courier for Napoleon before coming to England. It is an imposing building and occupies a prime position at the mouth of the river. Trade declined when the main rail link to Scotland over Shap was opened in the 1850s. It was used as a school for musketry reverting to hotel use in 1899.

5. North Euston Park Gardens.

The cannon on display is said to be the sole survivor of a number which fired a salute on the occasion of the visit by Queen Victoria and Prince Albert in 1847.

The stone block carries the coat of arms of the Lancashire/Yorkshire Railway Co. which took over the original rail link to Preston and dates from 1875. It was presented to the town by the Fleetwood Civic Society in 1976.

The obelisk is a memorial to James Abram and John Greenall who lost their lives endeavouring to save others during a great storm in 1890.

The anchors on display lay on the sea-bed for many years before being raised and put here in the park.

6. Fishermen's Memorial.

On the promenade, in front of the North Euston Park Gardens, there is a memorial to all fishermen who lost their lives fishing from Fleetwood. It takes the form of a trawler's gallast, the function of which was to stow away the trawl doors which kept the mouth of the net open when trawling. It was dedicated in 1987.

7. Queens Terrace.

Continuing our walk and passing the ferry on our left we soon reach Queens

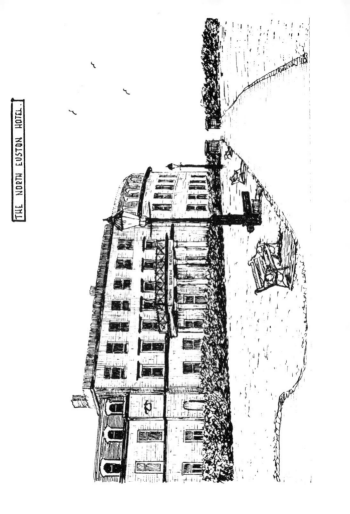

THE NORTH EUSTON HOTEL.

41

Terrace. These stone built houses were built in the Regency style between 1840 and 1844 for the upper class of the new town and for rent by wealthy holiday-makers. Sir Peter Hesketh-Fleetwood, Decimus Burton and John Abel Smith, a ship owner, were among the earlier occupants of these properties. They have now mostly been converted into luxury flats.

8 The Old Town Hall.

Further along Queens Terrace we come to a

terrace of brick built houses in the middle of which stands the Old Town Hall. It was built in 1838 as the customs house, used as a private residence between 1876 and 1889 after which it became the Town Hall of the Fleetwood Council up to 1974. After this date it was occupied by two departments of the newly-formed Wyre Borough Council until the new Civic Centre was opened at Poulton in 1988. There are plans to convert this fine building into a museum with the emphasis on the town's fishing heritage.

9. The Old Bonded Warehouse.

Continuing down Queens Terrace past the Steamer Hotel we reach Dock Street, along which we proceed to the junction with Adelaide Street. Here is one of the oldest buildings in Fleetwood; originally built as a Bonded Warehouse for the Customs Service, it is now in use as a shop.

10. The Whitworth Institute.

This building stands next door but one to the Bonded Warehouse. Built Gothic-style in 1863, it was named after Benjamin Whitworth

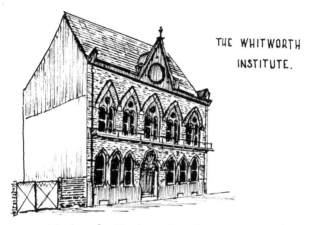

THE WHITWORTH
INSTITUTE.

a resident of Fleetwood and a Member of
Parliament. It provided assembly rooms,
reading rooms, a dance hall and facilities for
playing billiards. It became the town's
library in 1887 until the new library building
was opened on North Albert Street in 1988
At the time of writing it is still in use as
the Fleetwood Museum.

11. Fleetwood Market.

Returning to Adelaide Street we reach
the popular Fleetwood Market. The right to
hold a market was granted in 1275 to the

Manor of Rossall which included the land on which Fleetwood was built. The market was first opened in 1840 by the Lord of the Manor, Sir Peter Hesketh-Fleetwood, with the Local Authority acquiring the rights in 1890. It is open on Monday, Tuesday and Friday - May to October; Tuesday and Friday — November to April and on Saturdays and bank holidays — July to October.

12 The Clock Tower

Continuing down Adelaide Street to Albert Square we come to a clock tower which was bequeathed to the town by the late Mrs Margaret Rowntree, a former Councillor and the first Lady Mayor of Fleetwood. It was presented to the town in July 1986.

13 St Peter's Church.

Across the square is the parish church which

was built between 1840 and 1841 on land given by Sir Peter. It was consecrated by the Bishop of Chester on the 29th June 1841. Designed by Decimus Burton it is not considered to be one of his masterpieces.

14. St Mary's Roman Catholic Church.

Proceeding down Lord Street, which originally consisted of two parts – East St and West St, we pass the church of St Mary on our left. The foundation stone was laid by the Bishop of Liverpool in May 1866 and the church opened for worship on Nov 24th 1867. The architect was E. Welby Pugin and the cost of construction was £4,000.

15 Old Police Station

On the upper storey of the building now converted into two shop units Nos 125/127 Lord Street is the Lancashire Constabulary coat of arms, indicating its former use.

16 Mount Street Cottages.

Turning right up Mount Street we can

see some of the original town houses said to have been built to a design by Decimus Burton. Threatened by demolition, they were saved by the actions of the residents who refurbished them with Council assistance between 1982 and 1985. During the building work beautifully constructed brick-lined wells were uncovered containing remarkably clear, clean water. Additional new houses have been built in a style which complements the original dwellings.

To complete our walk we continue up Mount Street and Seabank Road to arrive back at the Mount.

A WALK FROM KNOTT END TO PREESALL AND BACK.

OVER GROWN SECTION OF TRACK.

A KNOTT END – PREESALL THREE AND A HALF MILE CIRCULAR WALK.

(Via two old historic homes and a disused railway track)

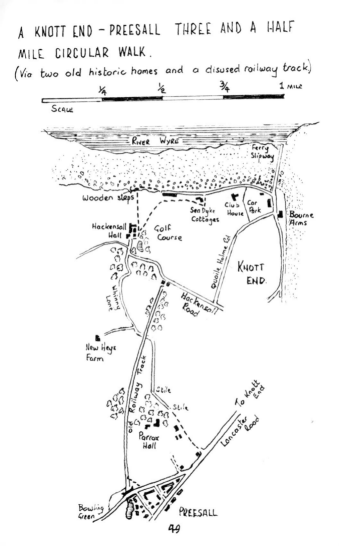

49

Our walk starts at the municipal car-park behind the café just past the Bourne Arms. The café is located in a building which was formerly Knott End station on the Garstang - Knott End Railway Line.

Leave the car-park and walk along the promenade, following the river upstream until the Sea Dyke Cottages are reached. To our right, across the river, the Port of Fleetwood and, on our left, the Knott End Golf Club course. The path goes behind these cottages following the edge of the course for a few hundred yards before crossing it, diagonally, to Hackensall Hall, or, carry on along the shore via wooden steps to the Hall.

SEA DYKE COTTAGES.

HACKENSALL HALL.

It is thought that the name derives from Hakon, a Norseman, who settled here in the 9th century. In 1190, Geoffrey, bowman of King John, received Hackensall and Preesall as a grant. Richard and Anne Fleetwood of Rossall built Hackensall Hall in 1656 after their residence suffered damage by sea inundation, unfortunately a common occurrence on the stormy Fylde coast. "God's Providence" and their initials are written on a date stone in the south gable of their new dwelling. It is possible that there was an earlier moated hall on this site before this date. During the 19th century considerable restoration work was carried out by Sir James Bourne, Lord of the Manor. Tradition has it that two concealed skeletons were found when walls were taken down during restoration and that the Hall is haunted by a ghostly horse.

To continue our walk we pass

HACKENSALL HALL.

Hackensall Hall and turn first left into Hackensall Road where we proceed as far as the first cottage on our right. This was formerly the level crossing keeper's cottage but it is now called "Woodside". The path goes between this and the next dwelling and leads us onto the track-bed of the former Garstang-Knott End

THE PILLING PIG

Railway which was known to the locals as the "Pilling Pig".

THE GARSTANG - KNOTT END RAILWAY.

<u>1864.</u>   Parliament Authority given

<u>1870</u>   Garstang to Pilling stretch opened
11½ miles - single track.

1876 Engine "Farmers Friend" acquired (sold in
      1883) had a whistle which sounded
      like a dying pig — origin of "Pilling Pig".
1880. Official receiver appointed.
1897. Company handed back to directors.
1908. Line extended to Knott End, a
      temporary level crossing being used
      on the Preesall-Knott End road until
      the bridge was completed.
1908-1930. Goods and passenger service.
1911. Branch line taken to the United
      Alkali Co. saltmine and jetty.
1930-1950.   Goods only.
1950. Knott End to Pilling closed and
      the track lifted.
1963. Pilling to Garstang closed and
      the track lifted.

The path follows the line of the old
railway for just under a mile until
the bridge is reached. Here we turn
left and follow a well-used path
up onto the road from where a detour
can be made by turning right up the hill to

the village of Preesall where refreshments can be taken. There are two old unspoilt inns, the Black Bull and the Saracen's Head.

To continue the walk we should turn left at the road and, going down the hill, carry on down the road until a road junction is reached just beyond the gate-house and main entrance to Parrox Hall. Here we turn left and, after a few yards, left again past the Medical Centre to take the footpath over the field. Passing in front of the farm and Parrox Hall, partly hidden in the trees on our left, we reach a stile in the corner of the field.

PARROX HALL.

The word parrox derives from the Old English word "parroc", meaning an enclosure or park. The present structure dates from the first half of the 17th century but an earlier building appears to have been on the site as far back as 1479. It has been the family home of the Elletsons since 1690 when

TRACK TOWARDS PREESALL.

OLD RAILWAY BRIDGE

John Elletson married Catherine Fyfe.

To continue the walk we climb the stile and on reaching, and crossing over, a second stile we follow the path which bears right and runs alongside a drainage ditch, eventually crossing over the disused railway track which we had previously walked along. Carrying on down the lane (Whinny Lane) we arrive at the junction with Hackensall Road and continuing on in front of Hackensall Hall we retrace our steps across the golf course to the riverside promenade and then on to the car-park, the start of our walk.

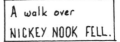

A walk over
NICKEY NOOK FELL.

NICKEY NOOK — A THREE MILE CIRCULAR WALK.—

This is one of the best. It has everything....
a gentle fell-walk; spectacular views; a lake (albeit
manmade) and, finally, a walk through a secluded
wooded valley back to the start.

It is a walk for all the family, young and
old alike.

Boots or stout walking shoes are the most
sensible form of footwear.

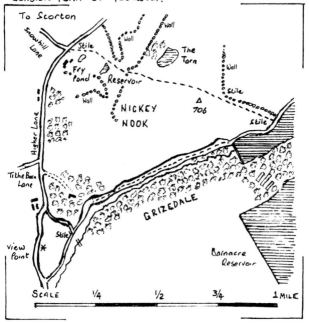

59

For the motorist informal parking is available on Higher Lane but please park with consideration for others. Our walk starts at the stile on Higher Lane opposite the junction with Snowhill Lane. Climb the stile onto the fell and after a few yards we pass the fry pond on our right.

The fry pond is manmade; evidence of the stone-lined banks and the sluice can still be seen. The pond was used for rearing young fish for the purpose of stocking the lake at Wyresdale Park, the water-level being controlled by operating the sluice-gate.

THE FRY POND.

Climbing steeply up the fell we pass a small reservoir on our right and, following the path upwards, we pass the tarn on lower ground on our left. The summit is soon reached and here we can rest and admire the extensive views. The Lake District mountains, the Bowland Fells and the Fylde plain down to the Irish Sea can all be seen on a clear fine day.

To leave the fell we carry on until we reach a dry-stone wall with a stile over it. Do not cross this stile but follow the wall downhill and pick up the well-defined path which takes us down to the Grizedale Valley. This path is steep, so take care! At the bottom we climb over a stile made of kerb-stones set into a dry-stone wall and turn right following the track alongside the reservoir.

THE TARN.

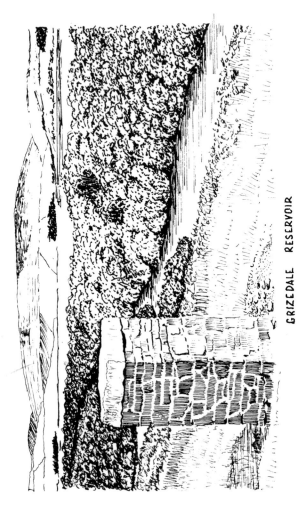

GRIZEDALE RESERVOIR

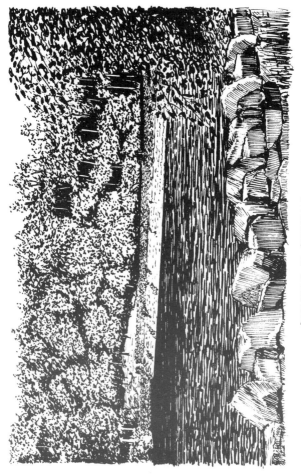

RESERVOIR IN GRIZEDALE.

The stony track takes us past the reservoir and then through a wood, a most delightful place, until we reach open meadows. At the stile a "short cut" can be made by taking the path to the right but our walk carries on across the meadow to join the metalled road – Higher Lane – where we turn right. The road climbs steeply and soon we are rewarded with a superb view of Grizedale with Nickey Nook Fell in the background. Carry on along the road to the starting point to finish the walk, which I think that you will agree, is, "one of the best."

GRIZEDALE

WOODLAND PATH IN GRIZEDALE

65

A WALK THROUGH BROCK BOTTOMS

BROCK BOTTOM — A THREE MILE WALK. —

Our walk starts at the carpark and picnic area map grid reference 549 431. Again you are advised to wear "wellies" or walking boots. There are plenty of parking spaces at the carpark and picnic area which has recently been

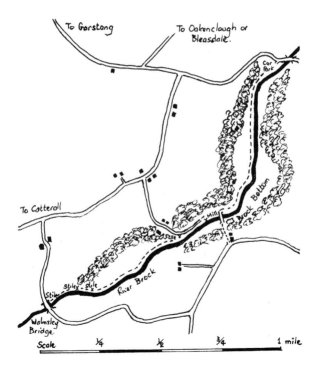

improved and developed as part of the Wyre
Borough Council's amenity schemes programme.
The work, completed in 1987, was carried out
by Wyre Community Services Ltd, which is
funded by the Manpower Services Commission
and sponsored by the Borough Council and the
I. C. I. p.l.c.

Leave the car-park and walk downstream
on the riverside path which follows the course

BRIDGE AT BROCK MILL

of the river as it threads it way in the steep-sided wooded valley. A nature trail laid by the Lancashire Trust for Nature Conservation can also be followed.

Crossing a stream the path continues through a meadow then through trees as the valley bottom narrows. Look out for the remains of a dam in the river. A massive concrete sluice can be seen, as can evidence of a now dry mill stream which supplied water to the mill pond at Brock Bottom Mill.

Passing, but not crossing over, the footbridge we continue until a path joins the main route from the left. This path follows the bank of the former mill dam to the ruins of Brock Bottom Mill and the remains of millworkers' cottages, all of which being situated on privately owned land.

The Mill

A mill was in existence on this site in 1786, referred to on Yates' Map as a paper mill. A three-storey mill, used for spinning and weaving cotton, replaced the paper mill in the period 1790-1795. This was burned down about 1860 and subsequently replaced by a two-storey structure. After a brief period of roller making, the mill finished its life as a file-cutting manufactory, closing its doors to production in 1923. During the 1930s the mill building was used as a tea-shop and dance venue the whole valley being established as a popular walking and camping area by this time. In the ruins of

the mill, the remains of the waterwheel and the grindstone used for making files can be seen.

To continue the walk we carry on down the main path until a stile is reached which we climb; the path then follows the river bank through the meadows. We cross a stream by a small footbridge then two more stiles before we reach our destination - Walmsley Bridge.

To return we can retrace our steps or, as an alternative, cross the Brock at Walmsley Bridge and follow the narrow metalled lane to a road junction where we turn left. Proceed until a white-washed cottage is reached on a bend on the road. A track at the side takes us down to the footbridge at Brock

Bottoms. Cross over the bridge to join the footpath which is followed upstream to the car-park and picnic area.

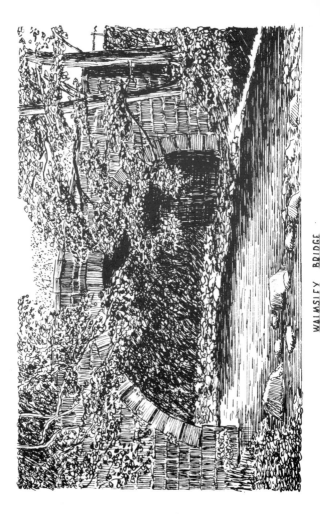

WALMSLEY BRIDGE

A GARSTANG WALK.

THE OLD TOWN HALL.

A GARSTANG WALK - 2¼ MILE CIRCULAR. -

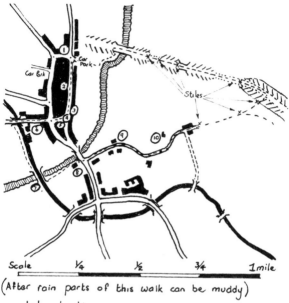

Scale | ¼ | ½ | ¾ | 1 mile

(After rain parts of this walk can be muddy)

Introduction

The Domesday Book records the existence of Cherestanc. The township was under the ownership of the Baron of Kendal and Wyresdale in 1226. From 1752 Edward Walpole and his descendents held the Manor. The Civil War saw the arrival of Cromwell's troops for the siege of Greenhalgh Castle. Bonnie Prince Charlie is recorded as having stayed here briefly in 1745. Stage and mail coaches stopped here on their route North and this, and the canal trade, brought prosperity. Garstang remains a thriving and attractive country town and well worth exploring.

The starting point of our walk is the car park at the Community Centre, the former District Council Offices. There are exciting plans to convert part of this building into a Heritage/Discovery Centre.

<u>1   The Old Grammar School.</u>

Opposite the Community Centre stands the Old Grammar School now the town's Art Centre. It was built in 1756 on land presented to the town by Sir Edward Walpole and ceased use as a school in 1929.

Proceeding left down the High Street, and, after a short walk, can be seen a

2. Horse Mounting Block

This three-step stone mounting block has some initials and a date carved into the stone;

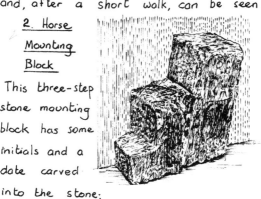

although badly worn, the letters R.E. RA can just be made out. The date is even more difficult to make out but I think it is 1685. As you progress down the High Street notice the weinds, old pedestrian rights of way, leading from it.

3 The Old Town Hall.

The Mayor and corporation of the town
of Garstang were constituted by Charles II
who, in 1680, granted the charter. The Town
Hall was erected in 1755 on the site of the
original building. It used to house the old
corn market and it contains a small jail cell.

The Market Hall, built in 1843, stands next
to it. The right to hold a street market was
granted to the Abbots of Cockersand in
1311. A street market is still held every
Thursday.

4 Market Place.

The cobblestones around the steps of the
market cross are the original. The cross
was restored in 1897, the previous one
being removed in 1753. In common with
many ancient towns Garstang once had its
own stocks but these, together with
some curved fishstones and the town
water pump, have, unfortunately, now
disappeared.

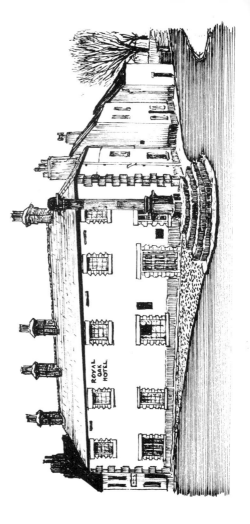

5   The Royal Oak.

This old inn was Garstang's principal posting house on the London to Edinburgh service. At its busiest the inn dealt with twenty-four coaches a day from early in the morning until midnight. During the siege of Greenhalgh Castle Cromwell's troops used the buildings on the West side of the inn. Sir Walter Scott stayed here and had the misfortune to lose two breastpins!

Turning right in front of the inn we proceed down Church St; passing the Parish Church of St. Thomas we reach the Tithebarn

6   "Owd Tithebarn."

This old building has been restored and is now in use as a restaurant. It stands alongside the canal basin, a very popular spot with visitors, and it houses a small canal museum which is well worth a visit.

We have to cross the canal over the hump-back bridge to reach the tow-path, along which we walk keeping the canal on our left. Soon we reach the aqueduct which carries the canal over the River Wyre.

THE OLD CORN MILL.

7 Wyre Aqueduct

This stone-built single-span aqueduct was designed and constructed by the engineer John Rennie and was opened for use in 1797.

We leave the towpath by the wooden steps at the side of the aqueduct and, walking underneath it, we follow the river passing the old corn mill to reach the road.

8 The Old Corn Mill

The Corn Mill was operated for many years by a local family, the Richardsons. The mill-wheel was housed in a stone tunnel in the basement and a stone weir across the river maintained a nine-foot water level which supplied the power. In 1961 the weir was destroyed when the river was in spate and the river returned to its natural water level. This fine building, now well restored, is in use as a rest-home for the elderly.

Having crossed the road we now proceed up the cul-de-sac, Castle Lane, and soon we are rewarded with fine views of the fells and the countryside. We pass a fine old farmhouse and cottage on our left.

9 Bonds Fold Farm.

This stone-built farmhouse and attached cottage, "Greenhalgh Cottage", are good examples of these types of buildings which can be found in these parts of the Wyre District. Note the datestone over the farmhouse door "1694 W.H."

Continuing up Castle Lane the ruins of Greenhalgh Castle soon come into view.

10. Greenhalgh Castle.

The castle was built in 1490 by Thomas Stanley, Earl of Derby, under licence from King Henry VII. It was constructed in the form of a square with a tower at each corner. Its presence contributed to the peace and stability of the surrounding country during those difficult times and remained until the Civil War. It withstood a two-year seige in support of the Royalist cause until it capitulated in 1645, the leader of the garrison having died and his followers becoming discouraged. By 1649 the castle lay in ruins, with the stone being removed for use as building material. Only the remains of one of the four corner towers survives to this day.

Continuing we walk through the farm at the end of the lane. A stile alongside a farm gate takes us into a field where we follow the fence until a stile on our left takes us across a small field to the disused railway cutting. Here we turn left and follow the track bed of the former Garstang and Knott End Railway — the "Pilling Pig" — back towards Garstang. There are more stiles to negotiate until we cross the river over the bridge where the flood control sluices are located. Leave the embankment by the stone steps and follow the riverside path around the cricket field to reach the car-park, our original starting point.

A WALK IN
CALDER VALE.

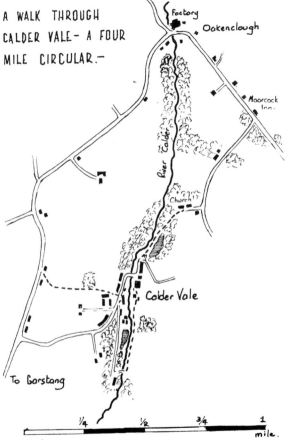

A WALK THROUGH CALDER VALE – A FOUR MILE CIRCULAR. –

Factory

Ookenclough

Moorcock Inn.

River Calder

Church?

Calder Vale

To Garstang

| 1/4 | 1/2 | 3/4 | 1 |

mile.

Scale

89

MILL DAM, CALDER VALE.

Calder Vale is a hidden village to be found at the end of the only approach road in a beautiful steep-sided wooded valley. Its terraced cottages cluster round the mill which was built in 1835 to weave cotton and was then driven by water. It is still in use for industrial purposes but power is no longer provided by the River Calder.

There is limited car-parking in front of the Methodist Chapel, the starting point of our walk. From here we pass in front of the stone-built terraced cottages of Long Row and through the gate to a tarmacadam path which skirts the mill dam and takes us through beautiful woodland. The path, climbing steeply, arrives at the church of St. John the Evangelist. Beyond the adjacent school a road junction is reached where we turn left and proceed to reach a metalled road and the Moorcock Inn. Turning left the road descends to the River Calder at Oakenclough where another large mill is now being used to provide industrial units.

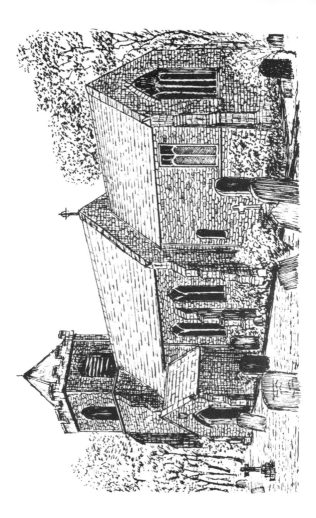

MOORCOCK INN.

RIVER CALDER.

Over the bridge we turn left and follow the road for just under a mile where it turns sharp left. About 650 yds. further on and passing a road junction to the right a bungalow is reached on our left. Here going over a stile and keeping to the right along the side of a field we reach a stile in a hedge. Over the stile we turn left and going over a footbridge we reach the next stile by walking across the field. Climb this stile and head across the field to the next. This takes us to a well-used path which runs behind some houses and leads to the road into Calder Vale via some stone steps.

Here we can turn left and return to the car-park or cross the road and take the track in front of the "Village Store" and some terraced cottages. Our route is along the track which bears right and, keeping level, passes in front of two houses before descending through trees to a footbridge high above the river. We cross the bridge and turn left following the river upstream and then along a path below a wood which takes us through a farmyard to the mill and our starting point.

FOOT-BRIDGE   CALDER VALE.

WALKS ALONG THE
LANCASTER CANAL.

WALKS ALONG THE LANCASTER CANAL.

Introduction

In spite of opposition the Bill promoting the building of a canal linking Preston, Lancaster and Kendal received Royal Assent on June 11th, 1792. The purpose was the transportation of coal, Northwards, from Lancashire and limestone, gravel, slate, timber and, sometimes, gunpowder on the return journey.

The total length of the canal from Preston to Kendal is 57 miles; the section from Preston to Tewitfield is 41½ miles long and is built without locks. This section was opened on the 22nd November 1797, the canal being carried over the River Lune by an aqueduct 221 yards in length. The engineer was the great John Rennie and the architect of the Lune Aqueduct was Alexander Stevens.

In 1819 the 15½ miles section from Tewitfield to Kendal was opened, with 8 locks raising the canal 95 feet.

The link to the sea, Galgate to Glasson, was

opened in 1819; it is 3 miles long and has 6 locks.

A 14 mile section from Preston to a point near Wigan was constructed but not connected to the rest of the system because of difficulties in crossing the Ribble. Freight was hauled over the unconnected section by horse-drawn wagon along a narrow gauge tramway. In 1859 this arrangement ceased and the Southern section was leased to the Leeds and Liverpool Canal Co.

By 1820 lightweight boats were operating an express passenger service in competition with the stage coaches. They covered the 57 miles from Preston to Kendal in seven hours, with the horses being changed every four miles.

The canal trade was affected by the opening of the railways and eventually, although a few coal barges continued, the canal basins at Preston and Kendal were filled in. In 1947 transport was nationalised and the canal passed first to the Transport Commission and then in 1963 to the British

Waterways Board. The building of the M6 made Tewitfield the northern limit of cruising.

Today the canal is managed for leisure and recreational pursuits such as boating, canoeing, angling and walking. Users are asked to abide by British Waterways bye-laws, follow the Country Code and share the towing path safely with others.

The Walks.

As the canal passes through Wyre it offers a unique way of experiencing the countryside without any worries of route finding. The information provided here, therefore, concentrates on matters such as car-parking and where refreshments can be obtained. Don't forget that 5 miles walked along the towpath means a round trip of 10 miles unless alternative transportation arrangements have been made for the return.

Sensible footwear is recommended.

LANCASTER CANAL GARSTANG TO BILSBORROW.
FOUR AND THREEQUARTER MILES.

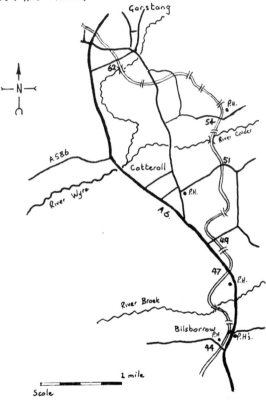

LANCASTER CANAL – Guide to Inns, Pubs, Cafes and Car-Parking:-

Key:
Br.	Bridge	
m.	Meals	
Tp/S	Tow-path side	
O/S	Offside	

Garstang.

Car-parking:- Two large free parks - High St and Parkhill Road

Inns and Pubs:-

Church Inn. Bonds Lane. Br 59; 220yds; O/S; M.

Old Tithe Barn. Canalside. Br 62; M.

Farmers Arms. Church St. Br. 62; 110yds; O/S; M.

Wheatsheaf. Parkhill Rd. Br. 62; 220yds; O/S; M.

Royal Oak. Market Place Br. 62; 330yds; O/S; M.

Eagle & Child. High St. Br. 62; 380yds; O/S. M.

Kings Arms. High St. Br. 62; 390yds; O/S. M.

Crown. High St. Br. 62; 430yds; O/S; M.

Cafes:-

Court Buttery. St Thomas Weind, off High St. Br 62; 250yds; O/S.

Coffee Inn. 46. High St. Br 62; 440yds; o/s

Post Horn Café, 19 High St. Br 62; 440yds; O/S.

Pine Kitchen Café, Oak Grove off Bridge St,
Br. 62; 375yds; O/S.

Wyre Café, Bridge St. Br 62; 390yds; O/S.

Catterall.

Kenlis Arms. Br. 54; 220yds; o/s; M.

Car-parking adj Kenlis Arms.

Brockholes Arms. Br 51; 2/3 mile; Tp/S; M.

Car-parking roadside Br 49.

Bilsborrow.

Green Man.   Br. 47; 330yds; o/s.

White Bull.   Brs. 44,45; Canalside; M.

Roebuck.   Brs. 44/45; Across road from
               the White Bull. M.

Old Nell's.   Br 44; Canalside; M.

Car-parking roadside, St Michael's Rd, Br 44.
or ask permission at Pubs.

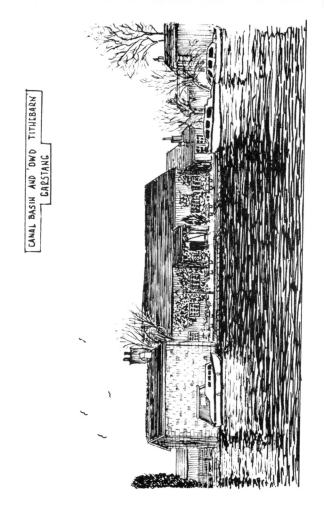

CANAL BASIN AND 'OWD TITHEBARN
GARSTANG

— CANAL AT THE BROCK AQUEDUCT —

BROCK AQUEDUCT.

OWD NELLS TAVERN. BILSBORROW.

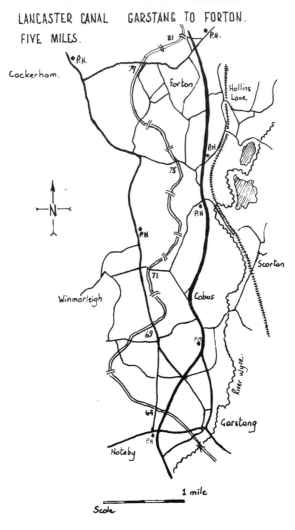

LANCASTER CANAL   GARSTANG TO FORTON.
FIVE MILES.

Cockerham.

P.H.

81

P.H.

79

Forton

Hollins Lane

P.H.

75

P.H.

N

P.H.

71

Winmarleigh

Cabus

Scorton

69

P.H.

River Wyre.

64

Garstang

P.H.

Noteby

1 mile

Scale

109

LANCASTER CANAL - Guide to Inns, Pubs, Cafés and Car-Parking -

Key
Br.	Bridge	
M.	Meals.	
Tp/S.	Tow-path side	
O/S.	Offside	

Garstang.

For details please refer to Pages 102, 103

Noteby.

Chequered Flag. Br.64; 220yds; Tp/S; M.
Cleveland Cafe. Br.64; 440yds; Tp/S.
Car-parking - roadside adj. Pub or ask permission for Pub car-park.

Cabus

Crofter's Hotel. Br.64; 1 mile; O/S; M. Left at X roads, left at and follow A6.
Car-parking - roadside Br.69.

Winmarleigh.

Patten Arms. Br.71; 3/4 mile; Tp/S; M. Right at X roads.

Cabus Nook.

Hamilton Arms.	Br. 73; 2/3 mile; O/S; M. Follow track over canal bridge, left at T junction.
Little Chef Restaurant	Opposite Hamilton Arms.

Forton.

New Holly Inn.	Br. 75; 3/4 mile; O/S; M. Bear left a road junction, left at X roads (A6).
Car-parking	limited roadside Br. 75.
Manor Inn.	Br. 79; 1 mile; Tp/S; M. Turn right at T junction.
Car-parking	Plenty roadside spaces Br. 79.
Bay Horse.	Br. 81; 550 yds; O/S; M. Over canal bridge, turn left, continue across main road (A6.)

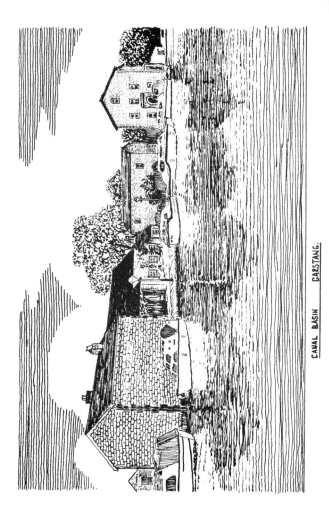

CANAL BASIN CARSTANG.

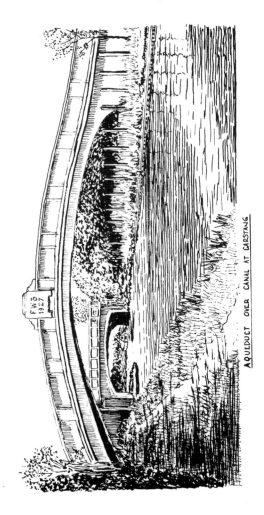

AQUEDUCT OVER CANAL AT GARSTANG

FWB
1927

BRIDGE NO. 69.

BRIDGE 79.

116

READER'S PERSONAL LOG

WALK	DATE	NOTES	WEATHER	START	FINISH

WALK	DATE	NOTES	WEATHER	START	FINISH

Other walking books from Carnegie Publishing

Walking from Garstang by Ian Brodie; new expanded edition of this extremely popular book . . . . £3.2£

Historic walks around Bleasdale by John Dixon and Jaana Järvinen – lovely walks with lots of historical information aswell £2.75

Historic walks around the West Pennine Moors authors as above, takes the walker into some of the most beautiful scenery in Lancashire £2.75

Rambling around Rossendale by Peter & Susan Lord. A brand new book for walkers of all ages and abilities. Great scenery with straightforward instructions £3.50

Historic walks from the Leeds and Liverpool Canal by John Dixon. Pocket-sized book full of picturesque circular walks starting from various points along the length of the canal £2.50

The Cistercian Way: A South Lakeland Walk by Ian Brodie, follow in the footsteps of monks in the unspoilt South Lakes . . . . NOW ONLY £1.99!

The above books can be bought from your local bookshop or newsagent or from:

CARNEGIE PUBLISHING LTD
18 MAYNARD STREET
ASHTON, PRESTON, PR2 2LS

(0772) 881246

All books normally despatched same day.